T0083458

12 women

an anthology
of poems

12 women

an anthology
of poems

Edited by Gerald Costanzo
Martha Paterson & Sophie Wirt

CARNEGIE MELLON UNIVERSITY PRESS
PITTSBURGH 2014

ACKNOWLEDGMENTS

The poems in this anthology are reprinted from the following books and journals:

Jasmine V. Bailey   *Alexandria* (2014)

Nicky Beer   *The Diminishing House* (2010)
The Octopus Game (2015)
"Relative State Formulation" first appeared in *Poetry Northwest*

Maggie Glover   *How I Went Red* (2014)

Heather Hartley   *Knock Knock* (2010)
"Jules & moi" first appeared in *The White Review*

K. A. Hays   *Dear Apocalypse* (2009)
Early Creatures, Native Gods (2012)
"And the Lord Hath Taken Away" first appeared in *Beloit Poetry Journal*

Cecilia Llompart   *The Wingless* (2014)

Bridget Lowe   *At the Autopsy of Vaslav Nijinsky* (2013)

Mihaela Moscaliuc   *Father Dirt* (2010)
Immigrant Model (2015)

Idra Novey   *The Next Country* (2008)
Exit, Civilian (2012)

Rachel Richardson   *Copperhead* (2011)
"Whale-Study" first appeared in *Michigan Quarterly Review*

Anne Marie Rooney   *Spitshine* (2012)
"What the Heart Recovers" first appeared in *So to Speak*
"But Animals Embody Gender Even As They Are Beyond It" first appeared in *West Branch*

Eleanor Stanford   *The Book of Sleep* (2008)
"Children" first appeared in *No Tell Motel*
"Two Common Daffodils" first appeared in *Drunken Boat*

Book design by Rachel Bullen and Connie Amoroso

Library of Congress Control Number 2014943681
ISBN 978-0-88748-592-3

10   9   8   7   6   5   4   3   2   1

CONTENTS

INTRODUCTION

One would like to suppose that an anthology containing poems by a group of outstanding women writers would need no introduction. Certainly it needs no rationale. The truth is the three of us—my co-editors Martha Paterson and Sophie Wirt, and I—were sitting in the office I have occupied at Carnegie Mellon for more than four decades, talking about poetry when we decided to compile this selection. Both of these young women were students in "Editing and Publishing," a course I have offered here since 1972 when legendary designer, art director, editor-in-chief and president at Harcourt Brace, and now literary agent extraordinaire Rubin Pfeffer was my first student. Through the years the course has produced a number of individuals who have made an impact on trade or scholarly publishing including Mary Alyce Reed, Jack Silbert, Vickie Stein, Alice Alfonsi, Laura Waldron, Allison Pottern, Matthew Kopel and many others. The most recent of these, 2007 graduate Michael Szczerban, after editing for Simon & Schuster where he received the 2012 Lawrence Peel Ashmead Editorial Award, moved in March of this year to join Judith Regan at her new publishing venture, Regan Arts, as Senior Editor. And now in October he has become executive editor at Little, Brown.

During the year Martha and Sophie were in the class, our conversations—beyond those concerning specific publishing projects and the reading of manuscripts—included discussions about the role of women in American Poetry, and whether women had received the acclaim their work seemed to us to warrant. I graduated from college in 1967, two years after the beginning of the period we now refer to as "The Sixties." In the writing workshops of which I was a member at Harvard and in graduate school at Johns Hopkins, mostly it was my female classmates who were the superior writers. It was not a situation to which we gave much thought; it just *was*. As was the gathering fact of feminism and the "women's movement." In the midst of great societal change over nearly half a century, where were those women who had been my peers? One hopes they became federal judges, teachers, corporate leaders, mothers in happy marriages, and so on. But it troubled me that I could not name one who had achieved any notice as a writer. Despite popular conjecture, perhaps women have not yet received their "due" in this field. Does the major prize in the genre tell us anything about this, we wondered. Since 1965, of the fifty-one Pulitzer Prize for Poetry winners, sixteen have been women (thirty-one percent). In the past twenty-five years, ten women have won the prize (forty percent). And things continue to improve: during the past five years, four of the Pulitzer awardees have been women.

Simply put, the twelve women included in this anthology are writers whom I have had the privilege of serving as their poetry (or poetry-in-translation) editor during the past ten years. While an editor remains certain of his (or her) taste in literature, one of my concerns in discussions with my co-editors was embodied in statements I've come across over the years by Ezra Pound, Richard Eberhart, and Donald Hall concerning the difficulty—even the impossibility—of being able to read and select the poems of poets in the generation which succeeds one's own, and indeed of each succeeding generation. This challenge has been both energizing and fascinating for me. During our deliberations, the three of us observed that some of the heirs of the New York School live in Paris, New Orleans and San Francisco; that Southern Writers are still "Southern" in even more intriguing fashion; that the West not only remains Wild, but wildly imaginative and profound. And while a Northern School of Poets has never been proclaimed, there is surely one now.

If my co-editors were charged with anything in the process of bringing this selection together, it was not to place themselves in the position of "women empowering women." What I hoped for was a monitoring of my editing style, and an exercising of their own critical acumen. I wanted an anthology of poems by women which was not the rendering of a man's idea of what women writers should be. I thank them for their efforts in this regard. *12 Women* is not only an *homage* to the talented young poets whose work appears in these pages, but also to the nearly four hundred students who, like Martha Paterson and Sophie Wirt, have worked in the Press offices gaining and applying their expertise to the publishing of books during my forty-five years as a professor at Carnegie Mellon.

We wish to extend our gratitude to Tom Hoeler for his work in the initial planning stages of this anthology. Thanks as well to Press Senior Editor Cynthia Lamb, and to staff members Connie Amoroso and Stacey Hsi; and to Vickie McKay and Eyona Bivins of the Carnegie Mellon Department of English.

—Gerald Costanzo

JASMINE V. BAILEY

Jasmine V. Bailey received her M.F.A. from the University of Virginia. She has taught English as a Fulbright fellow in Argentina and at Colgate University as an Olive B. O'Connor fellow. She has published a chapbook, *Sleep and What Precedes It*, which won the 2009 Longleaf Press Chapbook Prize, and her first collection of poems, *Alexandria*.

author photo: Jason Bailey

SUGAR HOLLOW

Tally the damages of our parting this way:
go to a swimming hole and take off your clothes.

Do this because I want to imagine you
breasting the cold water,

moving towards a fallen branch,
clutching it as you submerge.

Small fish will forget you
and dart around your ankles, a turtle will sleep

on the same log you sun yourself on,
out of reach.

You will not deify, you will not
alchemize—

you were already a god and gold;
I was there for it.

The mosquito net drawn around us,
time gave up freckling our bodies; I could see

you only, lit and dim.
In my mind you have always just finished

a handful of berries.

BOARDING SCHOOL

Owlets were moored in the distant tree.
Your down, your well-tended geese
and lambs that never grew.

You are where I have buried
the empty opera house
and whole forests. You I opened

like our clothes
to the wind's lunatic freedoms.
The clarinet it made of the merest Wednesday.

Perhaps you already knew
that no one can live
without disturbing the leaves.

STAR OF DAVID

It's true I've often left,
but never with your elegance—
tall, sad, carrying the one real kiss.
Who slept as perfectly in a heap of cans
or climbed the ski hill so sincerely?

You were lean as a smile,
slicing cucumbers, wilting lettuce,
folding jokes into your pocket—
your Star of David on my lips
or caught in hair.

After each blanket in the muddy town
has been washed and our footsteps
smoothed by runoff, your beauty catches
in my throat and I hunger after
forgiveness.

WILDWOOD

I required wine
and you brought two bottles to the beach,
where I undressed you

the common way—imagining it.
You lodged yourself
in the way of some fantasies,

blocking my view of the north side of Paris.
You were the color of almonds

almost burnt in a dry pan,
but you could not rival Paris.

DAYS OF AGGRESSIVE GEESE

On our bridge in Firenze, in the painting,
in the Renaissance, that cream morning,
sometimes you were Dante and sometimes
you were Beatrice. Sometimes I was the river,
sometimes the loose woman, and sometimes
we were both the blue friend looking on with
that unsettling face of discernment. Sometimes
I held a flower, gazing after my mother's window,
sometimes you put a foot out and held your heart.
Sometimes you held the violet and I my heart.

•

There were the people of God and the people
of drink and we were the people who wanted
to make Virginia like a winter jasmine open
in them. We stepped into your yard in slippers
and found a daffodil that meant to be itself in
a new way, to burst out of its own beauty into
another beauty. It was a loved thing, or at least
the consequence of a loved thing, as our gestures,
our pictures with the tulips, our showers, our weekdays,
had the color and scent and dew of loved things.

OBEISANCE FOR ANCESTORS

Perhaps if we dress in red costumes,
the dead will fear us for another year,
but I think color blindness
is one privilege of ghosts.

I didn't have my own dead, so I adopted.
The house is really filling up.
Each Thanksgiving is a struggle—

so much uneaten squash,
no one able even to locate
cranberries.

FOR HELEN

Broken moss on the bog where ghosts exhale
their threads to this world on the water's surface.
When the cranberries are red and heavy,
farmers flood the bog and shake them loose.

They float and are skimmed with great combs.

In this way I bring the knots out of my hair
grown almost too long to manage,
I would like a sister in these days to sit behind me
and with her fingers somehow make it right.

I wanted to look into the water cleared of fruit,
a bog or the sink where I've done washing,
where flecks of dirt swirl and settle
like dancers too shy to speak.

I wanted to find evidence of a myth
in my hair grown long, a dark red fruit,
the corolla of some flower whiter than its death.
The gleam of semi-permanence.

We went out in the wooden boat
onto the Great Egg Harbor in the rain
and caught bluefish, stripers, fished
until the camera had its fill,

tossed them back through the air like farewell.

EMPRESS, CONCUBINE

From the mess of the nightstand,
a chrysanthemum. No onlooker
to resent or illumine its beauty.
This quiet is the life to accept
as yours—even the bugs have shut down
in the October cold and you want
with nowhere to place it except holes
dug in the ground with a broken shovel.

No one examines what evening does to one
alone in the perfect autumn quiet.
Bring your wrong love and your one
bottle of whiskey. We will drink it
all the way out of the wizened city
back to where each other's presence
has confused us from.

FOR A TALL MAN

Not easy to remember old lovers
the mind has worn down like a coast—
what the inside of his wrist was,
how the ginkgos met over us some night
in yellow-green applause.

I've forgotten one who I once believed
would be my children's father.
Such bravado of a young woman—
each untried detail of herself insoluble.

DIAMONDS ON THE SOLES OF HER SHOES

We ended up by sleeping in a doorway. —Paul Simon

They were more ironic when we weren't in Williamsburg
or anywhere in Brooklyn, when for a decent slice of pizza
we might as well go to Naples, and the closest Jew
padded everywhere Saturdays chewing lavender pastries,
blessing the people in line for that week's two
forbidden films. You could see the impressions

they left alongside Amish horseprints and trace her direction
if you could follow the smell of voile. All the town's diamonds
came from elsewhere, not just the DRC; an Armenian jeweler
in Hoboken, a reviled aunt who died, a blustery proposal
aboard a cruise whose destination you're too dotty to remember.
She didn't have to put her feet up for you to recognize them:

every strand of hair, the useless belt, sun filtering
through Chinatown sunglasses, proved them, she just didn't need
what anybody had. Not the out-of-print book machine
or worried-over coffee of Soho, not the Bolshoi or Seine. They wore
like an Italian blazer from the eighties or a Kayan neck ring.
She tied a nylon around her cell phone and dragged it, crooning

Mapuche, saying, *It's me or it.* We colonized a swing set,
a gravestone, a stranded worm, broke into the First Madison Baptist Church,
the public library, the Korean nail shop, the Upstate Yoga Institute.
We demanded karaoke and refused to sing out loud, ordered Dubonnet
and threw the Drambuie they brought us at a cop. We made
off on someone's bike, getting a flat at the Elks Lodge where old men

smeared us with advice. She was a twenty-year-old man, she
was toothy, she was finite and hilarious. Steadily everything
became true, tinted green and yellow and see-through, then
evaporated in the morning before anyone had heard of coffee.
She was last seen slicing cucumbers, throwing ribbons out a window,
tapping out an old song with her moccasins, ruining the linoleum.

NICKY BEER

Nicky Beer is the author of *The Diminishing House*, winner of the 2010 Colorado Book Award for Poetry, and *The Octopus Game*. Her awards include a literature fellowship from the National Endowment for the Arts, a Ruth Lilly Fellowship from the Poetry Foundation and a Discovery/*The Nation* award. She is an assistant professor at the University of Colorado Denver.

AVUNCULARITY

Every child ought to have a dead uncle.
There should be only one surviving photograph,
or else a handful of epochal snapshots
where the face is always blurred, in half-light,
or otherwise indistinct. Much can made of
the raised glass in his hand and the quirked
corners of his smile. And who was that girl
standing with him? Ellie? Jean? No, the one
from Pittsburgh with the dogs.
You hadn't been born then anyway. . . .
This is the one whose fault it can be:
the slight warps, the spider-cracks in your speech,
the explanation for all of the wrongness
that made the other children pause, assess you
a little coldly and pull back as one toward the playground.
Why all of the strange words seem to rise
from your tongue like damp, nocturnal creatures
into an unwelcoming light. Why you insist
on that turd-brown jacket that smells like
a musty fruitcake. Why that one thumbnail
is always gnawed to a puffed red crescent.
This man will be your phantom limb,
the thing once flesh, thrust into absence,
now living as a restless pricking under your skin,
that inward itching, that impossible,
inescapable rue fretting to itself,
the way the mouth tries to form urgent words
in a dream. And you'll take out that picture
so that your eyes can retrace the details:
red shirt, a vague mess of books
and cards on the table, half of one silver
aluminum can, a bright nova hovering
over his left shoulder as though something
has chosen that moment to rush into his body.
See, see there, his buttons are done
wrong. He must have forgotten things
all the time, just like you.

MY FATHER IS A SMALL SUBMARINE

The hospital room at night
is the bottom of the ocean.
Knotted lengths of clear kelp
tether him to the bed,

and the electric thread of his heart
on the screen becomes a restless eel
questing the coral fan
of the horizontal blinds' shadow.

A half-dozen lionfish,
spines bright with toxins,
have the slow drift of deflating
helium balloons, their sides
inscribed with the rueful maxim
Love Me, Love My Danger.

He clicks the morphine drip,
counting off fathoms.
By dawn, a whale the size
of a house cat will have nestled itself

in the crook of his arm,
conjuring a song
he'll follow into a lightless trench,
a doorstep to the center of the earth.

BLUE THOUGHT/BLUE SHADE

Broad-billed parrot (extinct 17th century)

I flaunt a dense, veinal color, poised
on a bank drained to dull, iron-red dregs.

At my back, a purgatorial mountain
wraps its hips in orange mist.

A shadow cowers underneath my tail.

A mate, I think, would render me less
superb—though solitary, I am, at least,

singular. See how the scrub
nearly faints with admiration.

Every night, the same vision:
overcome by the weight of my head,

I struggle to keep the black barb of this beak
from piercing my own breast.

Every night, I watch
that implacable scythe sink

into a mass of indigo feathers and shear
painlessly through the ribs' curvature
to retrieve my heart,

shrieking back every word I'd taught it.

THE EXQUISITE FOREPLAY OF THE TORTOISE

Every movement of my body
is a genuflection to stone,
my flesh a chalice for dust,
which is itself the dry ghosts of flesh.

It is true that I have had
my dalliances with the odd
toadstool, the bulbous contours
of their weeping bride-heads,

but oh my love, consider
the rare patience of my desire,
the readiness with which my body
greets you, the anticipation

born in my clay heart
twenty-five years before
I could gaze over the horizon
of your skull, my two legs

trembling on your back
like a ship-born boy's
on his first beach, terrified
he will drown in this strange earth.

for Brian

BOYS IN DRESSES

Archival photograph,
Louisville Male High School Freshman Ballet, 1903
Australian Giant Cuttlefish (Sepia apama)

1.

Pubescent octet in sepia-wash, symmetrically posed
in borrowed frocks. Sausage-curl coiffure—wigs
on loan from the local Theatrical Society. A few passable
slippers in the front row, though one boy sports
his Sunday oxfords. The prima-Donald standing center's managed
to snag a proper pair of toe shoes, but stands flat-
footed, giving the lush ribbons crisscrossing his calves
a centurion gleam. His is the expression we most expect:
skeptical and detached, the barest smirk of compliance.
But it's the member of the *corps* in the upper left
that mesmerizes; while the other boys handle their skirts
as if plucking radioactive chickens, he outstretches his tulle
with a wrist meticulously arched. All of his angles—
elbow, hip, chin—are elegantly calculated.
Even his borrowed hair has an oddly sexual tousle.
He's not a handsome boy. The sharp, bladed column
of his nose draws the eye to the oblique tilt of his pout,
the unbalanced broadness of the jaw veering
into a too-narrow chin. But there's no mistaking
how the eyes smolder an invitation to anyone willing
to notice. *What you wanted doesn't matter*, they say.
What you'll want, in the end, is me.

2.

It's the sepia wash that's allowed them to see the century out,
that's kept their silver nitrate-dipped drag
from evaporating. The male *Sepia apama*, too, has occasionally
cross-dressed, though without an ounce of camp.
Here's the scene: one ample, alpha-male cuttlefish guards
his littler lady in a shallow seabed like a furious umbrella.
With gents outnumbering the dames four to one,
what else can he do? His skin glowers warnings

to the other males, stripes darkening and pulsing
the closer they approach the nuptial cave.
Sometimes they'll brawl, two Hypercolor tees
in a spin cycle. A smaller fellow drifts at a distance,
takes notes, waits for the loser to withdraw. He gives
his mantle a series of shivers, like a bedsheet snapping
leafy blotches of light on a clothesline, until he's draped
in a feminine damask of chromaphores. Flashing a dainty invitation,
he nears the big guy, whose body becomes an arched, approving
eyebrow in reply. He waves his sham-paramour in.
The back-door man becomes a front-door woman:
while the polygamist's gloating about his harem, the impostor
fucks the lady in the cave, who's more than game
to see what her new man's got up his skirt.

3.
Desire comes shaking its costume at us, laughing
at how willing we are to be duped. We've evolved for that, too:
the inclination to let pose and plumage lead us
into the undertow, the jagged, open mouth
disguised as a flower. But turn the voice-over down
to pantomime now. Let the rest be pure
choreography dipping in and out of shadows
that are live and hungry and expanding as a coral reef.
Sepia epicenes, we chase ourselves through your haze
of confounding ink. We don't want to be seen,
but seen through.

SKIN TRADE

". . . the real appeal of the show girl
lies not in her individuality
but in the way she is multiplied
and refracted across the stage."
And so you are not known for your-
self, but by your most convenient,
refractive metaphor: an abundance
of appendage. It is your gift
of chromatic mercuriality that goes
generally unnoticed, which is,
one supposes, your intention anyway.
As the occasion dictates—hunger,
panic, slow death—you become
whatever is appropriate, a perfect
black cocktail dress of predator/prey
in your effortlessness. Even while ailing
in your convalescent tank at the National Zoo
the aptly named Marcia Frame
could observe your skin dissolve
into "half ashen and half black,
as if some imaginary line
were drawn through [your] body,"
then pale as a Victorian neurasthenic,
then a ravenous terra-cotta,
all the while assuming "flamboyant
postures." Should we take this
as a sign of great compassion
or great duplicity? Think
of the marvelous homilies and clichés
that could have been! The un-
trustworthy would be *as consistent
as an octopus's skin*; a lost
cause would be *like trying to find
a frightened octopus*; the Dalai Lama
could urge us to adopt *the empathy
of the octopus* in our encounters

with strangers. But I'm content to cross-
reference you with *scapegoat, gull, sitting duck, clay
pigeon*: in mid-century *pulpo* pulp fiction
cover art, you obligingly incarnate
whatever terror the age required.
For the 1945 summer issue
of *Planet Stories* you were a mechanical
threat, incongruously sharp-toothed
and louver-jawed as a lamprey,
a bloodied and blue arm poised
to spank the barely covered bottom
of an alienne in heels with a geisha updo.
 In 1953's *Adventures Into the Unknown*
the mistress of the ostentatiously, insidiously red
menace attacking the captain of the derelict
fleet hag-cackled, "HA-HA! Now
do you know me for what I AM?"
Even this hour you lurk in the news-
channel slapdash as the roiling
embrace of coastal hurricane fronts,
the inky fire clouds shrouding the steel reef
of a city skyline, the viral naiad spiraling
in the blood stream . . .
It seems this is the most salient of all
your gifts: the sheer bonelessness
of you, how you collapse
and insinuate yourself into our most private
crevasses, feeding on whatever
schools of blind and blundering alarm
the sea change offers.
To know what you are
now, we must know
what we fear first.

GIANT SQUID CAUGHT ON FILM!

You spiraled to life in greenblack and white:
the same cinematic palette by which
we first watched the sex acts of celebrities.
We loved you a little less then, having
become unforgivably visible.
Even your conciliatory gesture
of self-mutilation, that orphaned
ticker tape arm hooksnagged, helloed and good-
byed by the current, could not mollify.
We wanted a mouthless god, eyes untouched
by light. Whose judgment was not judgment but
the pulse of instinct in a cold, dim mind.
Drag the camera down. Smash its aperture.
We cannot bear to have our depths unmonstered.

CRACKPOT ARCTIC OCTOPUS

I want to show you my blueprints.
This is where I'm going to put up the pistons,
The silver horses. I've been dreaming of
Building a giant carousel underwater, you see.

This is where I'm going. To put up the pistons
Close by the sea vents—risky, I know, but—
Building a giant carousel underwater! You see
Why it must be done. I try to keep calm,

Close by. The sea vents risk. I know but
Fucking and fighting in a green haze.
Why? It must be done. I try to keep clams
Quiet by drilling holes in their heads.

Fucking and fighting in a green haze
Will drive anyone quite crazy after a while.
Quite. By drilling holes in their heads,
The Eskimos released their demons into the sky.

Will drives anyone quite crazy. After a while
Down in the seabed it all became so clear to me.
The Eskimos released their demons. Into the sky?
Nonsense. They seeped into the ice,

Down in the seabed. It all came to me. So be clear—
This is not really what I wanted,
The nonsense they seeped into the ice,
Though I've made an amusement of it all the same.

This is not real: what I wanted,
The silver horses I've been dreaming of,
Though I've made an amusement of it. All the same,
I want to show you my blueprints.

RIMBAUD'S KRAKEN

Citizens, awake! These are not the low, mild
clouds of your usual daybreaks—behold
the slowly advancing arms of the apocalyptic
monster, already filling with a pink, sinister light!

The city is a coral reef flaunting electric crustaceans,
a lewd feast laid out for him under the heavens.
He will fiddle harshly the nude steeple of the church,
thump the opera house roof in a savage tom-tom.

His music will make the pauper priests and debutantes
run wild in the street, shucking moth-eaten cassocks
and silk-and-diamond unmentionables to careen
off one another like lascivious pinballs.

Look out, schoolteachers! He's come to suck the bones
from your bodies, to toss your slumping skins
like hobo overcoats into the gutters where you'll
spend your last breaths belching out chalk dust.

The savage urchins, those diminutive monsters
who set fire to the backs of stray dogs—
all at once they'll shriek in terror to see
their fingers turn to sardines in his thundering shadow.

The public monuments will swarm with snails,
their slime-trails a griffonage of queer divinations.
Don't bother running to the sewers to hide—
the pipes have already come alive in their catacombs, ready to strangle.

Citizens, it's all his! Your only chance now is to sprout
another quartet of limbs and clear the way as he unfurls
down the thoroughfares a hundredfold, while the paving stones
squeal like spinsters under the thick, obscene banners of his arms!

RELATIVE STATE FORMULATION

Say you're driving through a strange town, not strange,
really, but unfamiliar. Eventually
you'll pass that one particular house where
you'll almost stop, or at least briefly idle.
There will be something in the way the shutters
blister, how the late sun makes a parallel
blazoned pane with the door that will tell you
that this is the house of your other life.
The one in which you told him *yes*, in which
the branch did not, ultimately, catch her,
in which the storm kept your father from making
that train. You can almost see your red chair
in the living room, can't you, and the back
of a head you pray won't turn toward your lights.

MAGGIE GLOVER

Maggie Glover is originally from Pittsburgh, Pennsylvania. Her debut collection of poems is titled *How I Went Red*. She received her B.A. in English Literature (Creative Writing) from Denison University and an M.F.A. in poetry from West Virginia University, where she received the Russ MacDonald Graduate Award for Poetry in 2007. A four-time Pushcart Prize nominee, Glover's poetry has appeared in *The Journal*, *MANTIS*, *Ninth Letter*, *Smartish Pace*, *Verse Daily* and other literary journals. She lives in San Francisco, California.

author photo: Cheyenne Cary

CONGRATULATIONS! YOU'RE A GOOD PERSON

The transvestite said I had beautiful eyes,
wanted me to know that

all he wanted was someone to make him up
in the men's room and would I?

You hung around, your leggy self
always eager to help

the ones who need it
because it was your last night

in town and you hoped
the one who needed it was me.

It wasn't. We walked home
anyway, your big hands

searching for my little needs
and, when you couldn't find them,

you said: *Really, I've only ever loved you*,
and all I heard was the wind rushing, the cold.

AT 15, I AM AFRAID OF NOTHING

not the dead kitten in the creek,
not boys who pop my bike tires and,
the one who suggest the bedroom closet,
the quiet of his undoing (a lock, a belt),
not of no one noticing, not the dirt in
my face, the other boys at school,
not feeling

the romance of water to rib cage,
uncertainity like a bubble of gasoline,
his flute-shaped conciet, the carnality of
a circle, hooking my wrist,
the ache of my body's sockets,
anger and
its pressure,
the weight of it in my hand.

THE BOYS WHO LEARNED TO FUCK FROM PORN MOVIES VERSUS THE BOYS WHO LEARNED TO FUCK FROM THEIR FATHERS

One side offered, believe or not: daisies. Their orange bow ties and Monroe piercings made a hundred cities in the grass.

The other side: the knowledge of grasshoppers, how to jump rope—they wore sneakers that looked like sneakers, slogan pins like *Shy in the Tooth*.

The battle raged. After careful thought, I arranged for both teams to break my heart.

When I told them how, we were all surprised.

THE FIRST TIME

That night, we called it safe
to use nothing, as I had only skipped
one pill the week before. We were right.
The blood arrives as scheduled
while I watch my niece run backwards
for the first time. It isn't fear
that makes her laugh, sneakers paddling
without precision through grass,
but something close.

THE GARDEN PARTY

Lights bloom around my friend and me.
The hostess hands out small jewels of liquor.
Like all jungle dwellers, we are restless
to begin. We move through the glittery heat,
brushing through the feathered scarves
& vintage hats, seersucker and stripes.
An old woman tells us about her fear of little spaces,
how the world closes in, one breath at a time.
Oh, we say, *oh,* because we are still young
and the starlight sticks to us like spray paint.
The music moves us forward, *click-clack,*
past the paper lanterns & the clawfoot tub
full of bottles, past someone's red-eyed husband,
leaning against the wall. My friend snags her skirt
along a bench, ripping the hem.
Now it's a real party! The others move closer,
as bright and fast as flasher wrasses.
Someone sings out. The moon smokes around us
in circles—
      we are our own problem now.

POEM FROM THE HOTEL

Frustrated with my reform efforts, I gave up—
stopped tending to myself like an injured whitetail
(nursing the broken parts with a handkerchief,
a round of gauze to lift the ooze away from the body),
and mapped out my identity loss in real space,
like a blood splatter. The cold wind from the bar
window reminds me that there are still palm trees
in December, swaying. This means nothing to me,
Dear Reader. I am already aware of my choices.
I can care, or not care. I can wait, or not wait.
I cannot be armed by my secrets. I do not know
what they are. I can ask you for another chance.
This time, with a plot: a man walks into a bar.
He sits next to a woman, who is wearing only
one shoe. He asks her for a cigarette.
His blue eyes have blue eyes. She is already dead.
She gives him the cigarette, anyway.

SUNDAY, BEFORE GROCERY SHOPPING

The cat dips into the aquarium, paws
the old goldfish and you let her,
for a little while, pushing
another cold forkful of eggs
into your mouth. This is how you govern
your body, this and oily vitamins,
frequent trips to the Marine Park,
quick naps on the couch. You are tired
of waiting for me and I am tired
of waiting, hunched in the yard,
both hands in the garden, watering
the places where something could grow
if I thumbed them right, the hose quivering
in the grass like the snakes
we are both afraid of:
you, of their movement,
me, of their bite.

REPAIR

When my father first told me about the cancer,
I had just moved in. The landlord warned
about the tear in the screen, but I didn't understand
what such a snag could mean. For one week,
I watched the hornets toil a nest. Inside my window,
they built a home. I didn't stop them.
I didn't know how to begin.

ON RECOVERY

On his seventh birthday, my nephew's autism allows him
to enjoy the grass for hours in bare feet, like I once did
on Ecstasy, rolling in a field until, mud-covered, I told you,
"This is why people hug." He is busy in the daffodils
holding each unopened bud for moments when we call him
inside for the birthday cake. Its fire is, I imagine, a detonation
of color in his mind, blues and yellows pasting the ceiling,
and I'd like to think he squeals for this joy, realizing
a spectacle in this store-bought dessert, its curving icing
waves, its sugar pixels. My sister says it takes him
hours to recover from any emotion and I remember when,
after you moved out, I took him sledding on backyard hills,
how the ice hung from the trees like slender nooses
as he tossed snow into my face and, laughing,
I threw some back, punching a red button into his cheek.
He ran to the house, banging his fists against the window
until I followed and, not knowing another way, he hugged
my waist, screaming, "Angry, angry," and we both knew
it wasn't the right word, but close. We watch
the video of my sister taking him home after his birth,
and when he cries, she pulls him close, trying to explain:
"You were once that small. Once, I could hold you like that."

WHITE GOLDFISH
(A POEM OF THE FUTURE)

Another blackout, this one for days—

my daughter plugs in the lamp anyway,

preparing for the best;

pink shorts beam out.

She soaps white clouds inside the bathtub: *loop loop loop*.

She curls her hair with a big tin can.

She starts pancakes in the fire pit: *Look!*

Today, twenty thousand people died. A flash of butter,

a buzz of salt—

she moves the batter with her little spoon.

HEATHER HARTLEY

Heather Hartley is Paris editor at *Tin House* and the author of *Knock Knock* and *Adult Swim*. Her poems, essays and interviews have appeared in or on *The Guardian*, *The Literary Review*, *PBS NewsHour* and other venues. She has presented writers at Shakespeare & Company Bookshop's weekly reading series and writes a monthly column, "Apéritif," about literary Paris, for the *Tin House* website.

author photo: Vincenzo Giugliano

NUDES IN A NEW ENGLAND BARN

Suddenly, the barn fills with nudes.
They pour through the double wooden door, drop down from the hayloft,
climb through windows—pink impasto figures, fine fresco thin limbs, a baker's
dozen of breasts, rolls of pale green flesh or skin taut as stretched canvas, rough
and white to touch. Models thick as thieves everywhere you look.

*Ingres, stamping mud clots from his boots, ushers in two serpent-armed women, twins, in
turbans and with pale skin.*
Rubens' shy wife twists impossibly around herself, cornered in a fur wrap.
Delacroix's tormented women fall off of Shaker chairs, backs arched, onto
the barnwood floor. A titter rises in the room as bloody bloody Bacon drops
some screaming scraps at the door. Four models of Modigliani enter from the
left, hands linked, silent, proud, self-absorbed. They carry their flat beauty with
them as if on a frieze.

In the back of the barn, Jane Avril adjusts her stockings.
The three flaunting graces are there, La Goulue picks straw bits from her hair.
Paris sits in a corner judging. Toulouse-Lautrec's green whores mill around
touching their enormous hair. Elizabeth Siddal takes another draught of
laudanum. Two Austrian girls mutter guttural swears and curse an absent Egon
S., lover and depraved pervert extraordinaire.

Giacometti, worried, searches for Diego's head among the dung and damp hay.
He's lost the damned metaphorical thing again, and knows he must start over
from scratch—give the poor man another cigarette. Rodin knits his knotty,
plaster-crusted hands in his beard, unsure of what to do next.

Balthus watches the whole scene from a corner in a kimono, smoking, in dark glasses.
His matte nudes are cast against late afternoon light, a glow of green and red
tones. His girls leave a scent of apples in the room. Picasso, snug in the hayloft,
strokes his damzelles d'Avignon—he could give two figs. The ladies sleep on,
dreaming their Spanish dreams. Italian models, nameless, dot the room with
dark parts and loud shouts—you can barely stir them with a stick. Jeanne
Hébuterne, Modigliani's wife with the wild and soft gray eyes, throws herself
out the window to make more room.

Here, the scent of flesh overpowers any smell of paint, for there is a woman here—
behind the door, behind the canvas too—there is one even watching you. For
this is the largest retrospective ever—Italian, French, Goddess, Whore, Nude,
Model, Little Girl. Death and the Maiden. Wife taking a bath. Young girl with
arms crossed tightly across her chest. *La Grande Odalisque.* The painted, not the paintings.

The woman, the real one, unties her sash, steps out of her robe and
mounts the platform in the studio. (She's the one praying it will be warm.)
(She's the one with aches and pains and sighs, the one with tired eyes.) She
leads her still life the whole time the others have been making noise. You may
not know her name, but you will want to greet her anyway. She's waiting.

ADVICE FOR THE HIRSUTE

I've decided it's not a good excuse—
it could eat you for the rest of your days.

He never calls me bella. 'La mia ragazza,' etc.,
but it's been about three weeks now, or over a month,
depending on how you count—
(sex).

The lawyer has lost her mind but O can she dance.
For years, she didn't like her hands
but you can only hide them so long, I said, *a girl's only got so many pockets.*
(Now she's in love with them like a teenage girl.)

If I gave you the same gift again, wrapped differently,
but the same exact thing,
would you be happy again, a second time?

As kitsch as it sounds and as bad as the coffee is, that's how it goes.
You can only wax your crotch so long before finally, finally,
the hair creeps back like dark widow's weeds.

Now put on your words and go out and play with the other kids.
But whatever you do, for god's sake, don't congregate around
the toilets.

All year has been November—a little gray, worn out—Demeter in rags.

Yesterday, when she was driving, she said in the smallest voice,
What happened to my nice little life?
It was the most devastating thing.

It's like a cat with a sixth claw—
some things you just have to accept.

THIS HEART WAS MADE FOR STOMPING
—THINK TWICE, YOURS TOO.

—between Naples, Italy, the Loire Valley
in France, and the American Far West

I

We stole landscapes for hours.
Took pictures with no film in the camera.
Mistook local high school girls for whores.
Drove circles around Ballan-Miré—ghost town with a pretty name.
Listened to the theme song from *A Fistful of Dollars* a thousand times.
Drank our way through the rain in Tours.
Wore black and pretended to be dirty, dirty blondes.

II

Imagine yourself in a Stetson.
Your hands make a lariat around the small of my back.
Lasso me in, ride me long—
I don't know how to locate where we made love on a map.

III

There are many Wests
but there is one in the heart
rough and strange with no borders—
a wild place—
to which no one lays claim
without great tenderness,
without your
—my—
deepest consent.

RHAPSODY IN BLUE IN FRONT OF A
STATUE OF ALEXANDER PUSHKIN

—St. Petersburg, Russia

I

She works magic from the radius
of her Russian hips, pressing
blue thighs together, jeans grazing
the pavement—lusting
after Pushkin, pelvis to poet,
who from above demands with open palms
bread and butter, a pinch of salt, a breast—
something to cup in his oversized hands.

II

A bird perches on the poet's head,
women touch their hair on a further bench,
men smoke, read papers and roll cigarettes
and everyone seems to forget
the brash rhapsody in blue
with ferocious hips that rise and fall
in hopes of luring someone
into the trap of her looks.

III

Hours later, she's still there,
lingering and longing in the public square,
fencing thin fingers through long black hair
waiting for her own bronze horseman
or for any john to ride her away
from this midnight-blue fix
into the white nights of early morning.

BROAD STROKES IN A WINE BAR

The woman wearing green shoes is drunk. She laughs in lurid light, red head against a yellow wall, an ancient Bardot. Her teeth have a look of soft charcoal, her tongue a blackened wafer. She pets on men to offer her one drink and then another. The soft undersides of her arms are stained with Burgundy and gray. She tells her life story like a painting by Chagall—a violinist upturns a table on the ceiling, white brides float down dark corridors and red horses run as she runs and runs away, her feet stained with deep green grass. She's the portrait of Paris in the Second World War, she's what's left of occupied France.

RAPUNZEL ON AN IRONING BOARD

—for Carol Jean and Mary Jean

My mother and grandmother stand over the porcelain sink
with its long silver snout where water too hot or cold
streams out and onto my aching scalp.

The three of us are in the kitchen: red Formica, white sink, metal
ironing board.
Dark clouds of copper pots hover above my head.
Flat out on the board, my feet reach halfway to the end.

I take tight hold and grit my teeth and count:
one, two, three, four, knots, nails, snarls, ouch—
yes it's almost over yes it will end yes it will stop and not begin again

and then they'll wrap my damp hair in a big blue towel
and I'll be the queen of Sheba in my robe for an hour.

And they will smooth my hair over my shoulders
and braid little secrets into dark meshes
and I will have three guesses to guess their wishes.

And now, touching the crown of my head
or pulling back black loose strands
in the thick of my roots I still feel
the faint, leftover sting of their hands.

FOR DEATH AND THE MAIDEN

I
My grandmother bent over her bath,
flesh sagging, belly bloated, hanging—
her back soft,
strangely beautiful
as before.

II
A scar the length of an arm
from fingertip to shoulder,
straight as the letter *l*,
tender as a baby's eyelid purple and veined.

III
There is no *I* in death.
No vowel sound.
Just a pause between
the open casket and the dirt mound.

IV
The "o" in phone, in the empty room,
the open mouth, the dry throat.
Of calling out and no voice,
now, or ever again.

V
For what we wait for
this fall, no, this winter,
no, spring, snow
in May, no spring,
summer—while I'm away
in Saint Petersburg with its white nights
that do not sleep.

KNOCK KNOCK

He laughs little but makes others laugh.
—Anonymous

His fork outlasted his fuck.
His landlord was the king of butter.
His confidant the local barber.
He had a bitchy page.
Drank bitter bitters.
Knew a Senator who couldn't masticate.
Saw Padua from a pension.
Sérénissime.
There's a powdered wig and a mask involved.
A wayward monk and a wooden spoon.
An amazon in an auberge.
Macaroni, clitoris, ink.
A dictionary of cheese.
Candle wax and dead skin.
Flacons and tinctures and blancmange.
A singular gondola.
The Cabbala.
A woman with yellow roses in her gloved hands.
Someone's at the servant's door, someone's at the *porte cochère.*
Knock knock.
Who's there?
Casanova.

DRIP

Here comes my hostess naked with a wrench—
you could say it was Max's fault, Max, with a capital *M*—
it's his place on the *gracht*, his sounds in the night—
but between himself in Madrid and himself in that Italian villa,

we're back to the configuration of Nikki and me,
an art deco mirror, a marble bathroom,
and Amsterdam in November—
but this is all anecdotal.

Cometh my mistress bared, wraunch-wristed,
laurels in hair, she launches, forte and foretold,
into Maximilian's error with much ado—
Maximilian, with an uppercase *M*,
traipsing through the *gracht* at crepuscule
nick nick nick

All I was trying to do was wash my hair
in an apartment only an Andalusian woman could love—
you could say that was Max's fault—
his vegetable love for antique brass—

But I'm still thinking about her breasts—
how they looked like mine, but thirty years older,
lighter in color, same shape,
band aids, mirror, mirror.

This is my mistress of the housetess,
with the mostess, with the bustiness of a mousetess,
with four breasts between us and some ice water,
let me introduce you to myself, then—
later, older, saggier, and I think, most happier.

LE BÊTE HUMAINE

Past the café in the train station, the kiosk selling daily news,
whores selling their daily wares, men smoking moist cigars,
a train speeds on as its whistle screams
in a rush to arrive in Paris.

With no time to slow down, no time for time,
the train skips the tracks,
a screech, some soot, a lost shoe—
black arabesques twist in a grimace—
the train slams through the station.

A bookstall is hit—papers fly up,
penny dreadfuls rip to shreds,
words and love letters tossed with black soot,
books' spines broken, dust covers covered with dust.

In the rush, the well-thumbed faces of passengers blur—
gravel lodged in groomed beards, splintering glass,
a child's broken wooden whistle, blood on a bustle.

With a plunge as clean as an exclamation point,
la bête humaine rams out of control,
nose first into macadam, deeper towards dirt,
desperately back into earth

while all the time, a woman looks on, touches her hair,
a small boy throws a ball against a stone wall,
and somewhere a farmer continues to plow his fields.

JULES & MOI

Eighty percent of success is showing up.
—Woody Allen

A morning of tiles, park benches & sun, green, un-
aggressive in mid-year, with books & the runaway jury of girls
off to the Indian Ocean, Madagascar, to islands, Maurice, Reunion—
then the arabesques of black iron doors, 1 to 9 ABCD (you have to know), stun-
ning, this hour. That atelier is a red awning opening, *oh nothing*, beckon-
ing to an impasse where Jonathan, the ladybug, moves side-
ways toward Stanislas, just another name, proves
we are here, Our Lady of the Cars, the Fields—*Notre Dame des Champs.*
To stone columns, where Madeleine meets magenta, (church not girl, not
my runaway jury of girls) as clouds part to Madura,
we move closer to the sky's crux
up & back to where we began, unfamiliar, le Cardinal—sun starts
slanting by tables. This just happened: dreadlocks, and who
is Gus anyway & why isn't he here with us—it's the last cut of the scissors.

K.A. Hays is the author of *Early Creatures, Native Gods* and *Dear Apocalypse*. Her poems have appeared in *Best American Poetry*, *The Kenyon Review*, *The American Poetry Review* and many other venues. She currently lives in Lewisburg, Pennsylvania, and teaches at Bucknell University.

author photo: Carolina Ebeid

DEAR APOCALYPSE

Gust through—   good. Give us
over to the oaks,   sway the old
sheds, the mansions—   shake them down
to meadows,   unmake us, melt off
what was wasted   of our waking years—
but know   we're no worse
than former fools.   You could have felled us
a millennium back,   blasted and bludgeoned—
you're late.   Level us, but let it be
put in stone   (or penciled on plastic):
Here lie some bodies   who bear no blame
for any faults   the future may find
at rest in their ruins.   Remember: we had
a god who grumbled   through us, gave us
his face, held us—   fisted, we like to feel—
even as he ended us.   Excuse him.
He was, like any other man,   complicated.

IN THE GARDEN

Afternoons past three o'clock, the orchard shrugs.
The unripe apples look jaded and the air
tastes like fruit fermented. Afternoons
make us listless things, overripe. Why is it?

And soon the rattler, tomorrow, will swallow us,
its skin first gold, then brown, then shed. . . . Pluck,

heave me away to the compost. Afternoons I need
to talk epistemology with something ugly
and inanimate: the earth, for example.

THE WAY OF ALL THE EARTH
Joshua 23:14

In various ways we'll be taken. Fine, except

that we know it, and just when we've tricked it away

someone nearby—a sister, say, or a child—proves it again

as fact. More pleasant to be one of those turtles

who each September takes a last breath

and goes gliding down to the profound mud

to wag in for a fine six months of anti-meditation.

How brown it would be,

and more than milky, an opaque shell

around the shell of the body, any minnow who passed

taking the body for rocks that had sat on the bottom

for centuries, mossing. We would not attend

the last rites of our families. We would be happy

as stone until spring when we swam upwards

to catch ducks in our snappers—

oh, unavoidable affront, especially

for the old, for whom death's quick mouth

darts daily through reed and shallow pool.

It snatches from the surface the children

and sleek teens of the past, each month a volley

of funerals, leading up to the snap over a webbed foot,

when the self, which quakes and rages, is dragged under

until it is drowned. Better, perhaps, not to go

alone, but to pile, instead, like other turtles

on top of one another in a river's trench—

to stay alive by being nearly dead.

When the winter of dust

blustered sixty-four million years back,

and the great beasts who stalked the land suffered

and fell, their bulk heaving the hills—

all of that was only a loud game of billiards

to the turtles, who sank down away from the light

and let the arms and legs float in the waters,

each belly atop another shell, the skin assuming

the work of the lungs, so the lungs—

as the earth above wasted and tore—

might, through that din, be still.

THE LABOR OF WAKING

Difficult work. For the man who falls out
of mass migrations, waking
to a cot in Kazakhstan, for the woman who can wed
sleep as salt weds water
but rises for the graveyard shift, for all six billion of us

meandering wakers, tongues

ballooned beyond speech, seeing in sleep
a side of things more greenly,
where a room's wrought
in bolder hues, and seethes with meaning, it is difficult.
Of course, we must pretend

it is easy, must cast off our starred coverlets

as if they were nets, flop out
onto the cold floor. We must not unsettle
the dog, we must not cry—
though there was a first waking, a tumbling and splitting
where we were permitted to show

the gut urge, our hatred for being here.

Then we had purple faces,
clenched fists, closed eyes, the most perfect wail.
To give back an honesty to things
we would, the six billion of us, each day wake with the visible
signs of our horror, slick

with the fluids of elsewhere—and dream, a great placenta,

would fall out with us, baggy
and black, deflated on the floor.
Some spirit of good would swab and dress
our bodies, would take photographs:
the puckered lips, the dark tomato faces,

our wrinkles, little nowheres

from the nowhere we'd been.
We would gurgle, not yet knowing
those valleys where many walk,
the pits into which the awakened fall,

that there will come so many terrors to us

and to our measured hours.
Or that, after many mornings, many days,
we would come to love
this waking life enough to dread its loss.

IMAGINE HOW EASY IT MUST
BE FOR WEATHER

It's enough to curdle some jealousy in we humans—
saying we're fine, as dull
as blue skies in children's drawings,
white space between us and the spiky grass—
it's a shame we couldn't choke the worms out of the mud
as signs to one another, little hints.

And now the worms wallow up, ridiculous
as the insane, who have permission to go naked.

Surely we all fear the reach of madness.
But what if it made us as confident as the wind billowing
a hurricane, far past the flat snare of beaches,
over the triangle where ships go off radar
and laws get sucked down?

Let's say we could cook in the slurried waves,
spitting out the brack in us,
permitting what's necessary. Imagine that:
doing what conditions urge.

OF NATIVE GODS

Even the skin of the miracles
someone once frescoed
on the portico walls
lifts off—and still,
some men and women stand
beneath the whitened shapes
where towers were,
and I am no longer sure
whether all this might be intended
as miracle, or as mystery.
A real woman
smacks a boy's real cheek,
and the boy turns
towards me—
we too seem
to be standing
around some bleached-out miracle,
some monolith
no longer here.

TO THE VIRGIN, ALREADY ANSWERED

As the gulls that drift
with foam, the gulls
that sleep and beat off
as though the shales
threw them, or as
the shales themselves,
soon covered, soon exposed—
as anything that hovers
and flaps, waits and lets go,
hold us as dear as that:
as the mad eagle diving in cold,
and as the fish she's caught,
dumb, shock-mouthed,
speared, and finally aware.

AS SLEEP COMES, THOUGHT

They ride the cowlicks and manes of breezes, the swallows,
combing the air they fray, or kicking up a curl of wind,
their beaks parted, dusky insects gliding toward their throats
and into a longer night than they'd intended. But no more thinking
of the unsatisfied intentions of bugs—an excruciating,
ridiculous habit. Think of the swallows whose coats dampen
when they rush over the lake, so they perch in a low tree;
their gathering of white blouses and nervy iridescent cloaks,
their reckless arguments, their group preening and shuffling,
and how several share a slender twig without its cracking

seems the ideal situation,

one I'd take for myself, a black tree with ten or twenty others,
some digging at a wet breast or looking at a hazy mob of bugs,
two wrestling in air and clicking out a low mutter-song,
that song as common as the singers or as the dandelions,
now yellow pom-poms beneath a swallow tree, now gray haloes
taking leave, no buggy intentions there, no music, but causing the same pain
for which I hold thwarted intention and communal song responsible—
the quick unmarked succession of flowers, which become migrant bits
like bugs among the swallow hordes, maybe fooling one; think of that,
a quiet weed, drifting through its afterlife, may fool the birds.

THIS IS MY BODY IT WILL BE GIVEN UP FOR YOU

I have been watching the slurp and frolic of a wake
on the island's banks, the land's heckled edges

feeding the lake clay pies, meringues
of grit. What skin says

to the skin it rubs—this is my body
given—so says dirt to water, wing

to air; so says the overhanging birch
when the leaves have just busted out

of their tombs and look down
at the lake's stammer,

at first glimpsing their whole tree
silhouetted, then seeing through themselves

to the sludge of gray-green leaves that waffle
and blur on the lake-bottom,

a hundred seasons sucked down there,
no leaf alone, and all at ease—

a single wafer
on the same untasting tongue.

AND THE LORD HATH TAKEN AWAY

The bee claws into touch-me-nots,
the mouth a flame against the orange of it.
And the mind stops its minding.
The legs hold up the butt-end
to the flower. *Why not stay?*
the bee asks as the dusk comes.
Why not stay inside the orange mouth
above the fleabane, balling up
inside a horn of plenty. Mornings I find
such bees. Half in, half out.
The body in the mouth from which it drank.
Morning night-damp still. I shake the bush
of touch-me-nots, I make a blaze of them
against the cold. The bee holds fast, is drunk.

CECILIA LLOMPART

Cecilia Llompart was born in 1985 in Rio Piedras, Puerto Rico. Her ancestors are predominantly sugarcane growers, tobacco factory lectors, and self-proclaimed social revolutionaries. She received her B.A. from Florida State University and her M.F.A. from the University of Virginia. Her debut poetry collection is entitled *The Wingless*. She doesn't consider any one place home, preferring to think of herself as a traveling poet who belongs to the world and of poetry as a thing that belongs to the people.

author photo: Marcella Marie Gettel

Consider, O Lord, how You sit   atop the sky; like a man
                                                                    in a glass-bottom boat.

                    Consider sky elsewhere; worn thin as a mattress.

          Consider the women, marbling
                                                        in their corners
the men with tongues of bronze; how

                              you tool the silence around them.

Consider the rolling wheel of Spring
                                        the Summer, a haunt of blue;

                    How the rivers roll up   like prayer mats.

Consider my Lover;
                    the yellow church of his skin, the clean
          wells of his ears;

How the notes of a song come to him
                                                  like birds descending
                              on a power line; How

          in his absence   I am of two throats

                                        each of them cramped.

Consider, O Lover, my throat
                            white as cigarette paper.

The crushed lavender of my knuckles.

      My heart, a dulled   needle threaded through
                                    too many patterns.

            Lover, they were stitches of pain
                              you undid me of;

      There is blood gone rancid in me   you can not move.

But how we comb   and comb the night for jewels
                                          to stack
                                    around one another,
                  to cast in the mold of our love.

      That dandy, the sky, enters blue-suited
                                    sun like a scotch in hand

                  as I consider the brevity of a lion;

            How many flies can touch   at decay.

Consider the road, long
                  and forked as the Devil's own tongue.

      Consider the Devil, burning   every bridge;
                                                Placing
                        in every tree a black

bird.   In every bird a black   thought.

WHAT MY LONELINESS DOES

Pace sideways, on
pointed crab feet.

Skin me. Like the quick tongue
of a hunting knife.

Curl the floorboards.

Open like a sail and let the wind
fill it, like a man given to belly.

Migrate through my body,
to its warmer parts.

Wear the mouth of a blow-up doll.

Father the bees.

Grow roots, then teeth.

Like the snow, blanket
softly everything.

Unfold the days. Fold them
up again into paper cranes.

"BLESSED ARE THE WINGLESS . . ."

Blessed are the wingless, for their bones
are not hollow but heavy with want.

Blessed is whatever flocks homeward,
as well as whatever remains—as I do—

for the winter. Blessed are those who   5
shoulder up. Blessed are those who suffer

no fools. Blessed what is in me to tip
the intimate scale of guilt, and blessed

that guilt for it knows no immediate
bounds. For it made me better than I am.   10

Blessed is the solemn animal that weighs
every question asked, finally, by the river.

Blessed all the debris that waits inside
of monuments. Blessed is your body,

big enough for the both of us. Blessed   15
are my hands for falling upon all which

they do not understand. Blessed is the moon,
bled white, bandaged in silk. Blessed too,

the stars. For it is with the mercy of carrion
birds that they dip their fingers in silver

and pick her carcass clean. Blessed is the sea, 20
graveyard of time. Blessed are the black waves

that congregate like mourners. Blessed are those
who have done their weeping, and are quieter now.

SUNDAY

Little harder getting up today but you do
and at least the water is warm at least there's
time for more than toast. You're one boot in
when the boss calls it's a good boss you have
now and everything is fine just have the day
off no you've earned it. The day begins to
unlock its possibilities for you and breakfast
is a little cold by now but the coffee is just
right and you let the dog clean the plate and
the dog knows this is a treat and looks back
at you with a grateful way and a mouthful
of egg. And you know that you won't need
a cigarette today won't need to soak your
feet won't curse your back. And if the leaves
need raking you are glad to rake if the boy
and the ball you are glad to throw it and there
is a book you will be glad to sit with on a day
like this you are even glad for God's many
creatures the deer the crows the mice the flies.

FEBRUARY

The year begins underground, in a cradle
of worms inching toward more rain.

February, violin-shaped, drops without
a sound from the tangles overhead.

The night is black and flat-backed,
a scorpion carrying diamonds, and

the moon poles a slow gondola around
the stars—each a naked woman bathing

in dark waters. I know my breasts, small
as plums, would win no blue ribbons.

But in your hands they tremble and fill
with song like plump, white birds.

SEPTEMBER

September fills the house with papers
until you've lost me under them.

Our ceiling is milk-colored
and our windows wear the sunlight

like a borrowed necklace. Your hands
are simple and birdlike. They open up

a window in the sky and pull the morning
down from it. Morning cups around

our white house, like your hand
around my breast, and warms it

all at once. When I leave the bed,
papers will scatter—reshape the floor.

THIS IS WHAT HAPPENS

When my mother enters the room: all of the doors
disappear. When my father enters the room: he walks
back out of it. When he enters the room again: I see
a man who values much, who does not always know
what to do with his hands. When my grandmother:
skies and skies and skies of soft-colored birds. When
my grandfather: these birds begin to fill the trees.
When my sister: these trees bear sudden fruit and
the fruit never falls. When a preacher enters the room:
We all stand up a little straighter and let him have
a good look at us. Then we bow our heads and have
our separate thoughts. When you enter the room:
the tightest parts of me soften. The softest part of me

hums.

"THERE IS A LIGHT . . ."

There is a light that never went out. I know this now.
Listen, you are that light—and it is your own cadence
at which you wonder, lavished upon the face of another.
It was in you that hope was housed and from you that it
is now forged. You are this final and most welcome wind
in the long game of sails. See how even the pelicans have
drawn near. You touch each thing with your gentle hands
and with precision. And though you marvel at these ships
come homeward I tell you—it was always you drawing
up the anchors and moving them along. This much I have
learned. That a line of poetry can drape itself over all other
lines like the tide running all the old names out of the sand.

That it all leads us to the sea.

"THIS IS NOT A VIOLIN . . ."

This is not a violin. It is not tucked
under my quivering chin. I am not
eleven and my eyes are not closed.

The bruise on our father's arm
does not startle me because our mother
would not bite him there. I do not

hear the fist at my door. I am not
kneeling in my closet, I am not
wearing nothing but a towel.

Our mother is not down the street
in a nightgown. Our father did not
just run after her and he did not leave

the front door open. The neighbors
are not calling. My sister is not looking
up at me, so I do not have to pretend

it is going to be fine. It is not two
in the morning. This is not the tree
I have climbed, it is not dark and

it is not raining.

BRIDGET LOWE

Bridget Lowe is the author of *At the Autopsy of Vaslav Nijinsky*. Her poems have appeared in *The American Poetry Review*, *Ploughshares*, *Best American Poetry*, *The New Republic* and *Parnassus*, among other publications. She is the recipient of a "Discovery"/*Boston Review* prize and fellowships to The MacDowell Colony and the Bread Loaf Writers' Conference. She currently lives in Kansas City, where she was born.

author photo: Jennifer Wetzel

POEM FOR VIRGINIA AS JOAN OF ARC

In the form of a voice that hated you
your counsel came.

You lowered yourself
to the bathroom floor to hear it.

The world went slow as a drip of something
sugared. You couldn't speak

clearly. You stumbled over birds.
The call of God is gradual.

Alone you stood and flickered in the kitchen,
alone you stood on stage.

The dog stepped around you,
the television throbbed

a bruise-colored comfort, beacon for your bed-boat.
In the basement your father's waders

hung on a hook and, even out of water,
held the shape of a man.

You held the hand of a windowpane
and what sights it showed you, things it demanded!

When the time came to confess
what you'd seen a doctor was called

to hear you out. You were doubted because
you did not play at recess with the other girls.

You did not put flowers in your hair
or call a man a god.

AT THE AUTOPSY OF VASLAV NIJINKSY

They sliced the soles of his feet
open, lengthwise then crosswise

to see if there was some trick,
an explanation

for the man who could fly,
the man who saw the godhead

with his naked eye.
They pinned the flaps of skin

open like wings
and searched inside the gristle

for a machine,
a motor and spring, the wheel

inside the bone, the reason
why.

He must have been playing
a trick on them

all this time,
the wool pulled tight

over the collective cyclopic eye,
flashbulb-bright—

he must have, he must
have lied.

But the foot was that
of a normal man

after all, after all that
and they sewed the foot together again.

PORTRAIT OF YOUNG SUBURBAN MALE AS
THE WILD BOY OF AVEYRON

As a teenager he would touch girls in their sleep.
Their bodies gave off some kind of heat
he sought.

His hands were dumb instruments
as he put them underneath their acrylic nightgowns,
compasses and protractors, things

bought to start the seventh grade
but never used to measure anything.

He would feel the ridges of their ribs
as he dragged a fingernail lightly across the skin
then down to the new hair

which he took as proof that everyone
was an animal somewhere.

Then in the morning he would wake for school
and the moon would be gone.

LEITMOTIF

I was devoted, I sat at your feet.
I called a photograph of a telephone
twenty times a day, asking for you, for you, for you.

I wore your ring until my hand fell off.
I put my hand on ice, my body under glass.
I slept a hundred years like that.

People came from distant lands to admire me.
My hair was preserved, a single flame.
Where were you?

When I awoke, I met a statue with your face.
It was as if no time had passed at all.
I bowed. I began

a polite conversation about weather.

ANTI-PASTORAL

Your green Arcadian hills do not interest me.
The bird-bright eyes of every bird cared for,
the way it is promised, the way it is written,
everyone fat on their share of sun and seed.

But I don't see you in the dark streak of a cat
crossing the street or the regal skunk in summer's heat
that strolls the sidewalk after dark, stopping to look at me
before moving on to its home under a neighbor's porch,
pushing its black-white weight through the latticework.

I don't see you in a head of lettuce, decapitated
and wet at the grocery store, singing in Orphic dissonance.
I look at your trees and see the night my mind rose up
and left the body's bed, the skin of the moon
in your teeth.

I begged you to make the mule of my mind
come back. Do you remember what you said?
Nothing. And in the silence after that—
my head without my body, singing on the riverbed.

THE FORGOTTEN ACTRESS HECKLES AN
IMPORTANT MAN AT AN AWARDS DINNER IN L.A.

You felt impatient. There were so many things
to eat there. And everyone kept raising their
drink. All hail someone or something! So you drank
until the room came into focus in a kind of
internal way. There were so many people there
in suits and dresses. What did they want?
You had not eaten in days. You knew that
most of what came out of a mouth and, conversely
what went into a mouth, was bile. Most days
you tried to turn your mouth into a brick wall.
You focused on not moving your tongue
into crevices, dare it exercise the muscle or find
a morsel. It felt like purification, it felt so sure.
Then you opened your mouth like a door and stepped
through into the fire (how it poured!) until
you were carried out of the ballroom by your elbows.

GOD IS A MATHEMATICIAN
AND IN MY DREAMS

God is a mathematician and in my dreams
I'm held down while my head is wrapped in netting
and strangers lick between my legs and laugh.
Then my legs are bent into various triangular shapes
and their degrees measured and recorded with tiny pencils
and photographed for an award-winning textbook.
Only a mathematician would let that happen.
Only a mathematician would force me
to the front of the room when I didn't know
the answer to a problem, thereby requiring me to draw
a picture of the male anatomy, bulbous and hairy,
in order to maintain my pride, control, and honor. I rode
your 8th grade chalkboard like a fucking horse, my horse,
my stallion, and even today, Mr. Company, I reject
the equation you have left like a week old dinner
for me to eat and eat at your wicked and loveless table.

PRAYER

Bend me so my filth is most apparent.
Stretch me past the point where flesh still gives.
Give me all the things I never wanted.
Save me from this strange and loveless thing
I've become. Perfume me with the oil of the sorry.
Help me to be eager for the white-hot whip
of heaven, for the thunderbolt, for the reins
you hold in earnest do not hurt me.
I don't deserve the reins you hold in earnest.
Is it you who will keep steadfast by my side?
The arrows fly. Meanwhile the bird watches,
a thousand tricks in its black, million-sided eye.
I moan, I beat, I tear my garment in my
heat, in my love, O Lord, your name is like a bird
to me, your name is like a bird which imitates
but does not truly speak.

A WASHERWOMAN'S ACCOUNT, AVEYRON, 1799

At first it seemed a beast, backward
in its way of walking, with a wild beard over half its body
as its limbs moved wrongly through the trees.
I looked for wings or beak but found him standing
on two feet, more like a man than not.
Sunlight was coming through in places
so that his face was briefly shown to me—
a fruit fallen and then trod on,
raked by birds and vermin for the seeds.
When word spread of what I'd seen
I was asked to tell my story in a formal manner
before a team of doctors and officials,
for a written account to be published in some kind of paper.
Instead I told them it was an ordinary day
and that I had simply wanted some attention
from my husband, who lately has been
eyeing other women, and so
had dreamed the creature as a way to turn his head,
if only for a minute and out of pity.

EAT NOT THE HEART, NEITHER THE BRAIN

Or eat the heart but salt it,
Roll it in the spices because how very bland
it has become in the unending filth of your hands.
But save the brain.

Or eat that too but know that it will be cool
and heavy on your tongue
and capable of great calculation.
It calculates your beastliness as you eat.

Eat them both undercooked, without silverware.
Or sauté them in butter and garlic,
coaxing their bodies, snail-like, from my
carcass. Slide them like oysters

into the dank cave of your mouth.
Light candles, wear a suit.
Put a roof over their heads, promise
each the biggest bedroom.

But listen to me when I tell you
the soul is something best avoided.
Or don't. Who am I
to warn of what you'll suffer.

Mihaela Moscaliuc is the author of *Father Dirt*, which won the Kinereth Gensler Award, translator of Carmelia Leonte's *The Hiss of the Viper*, and *Immigrant Model*. Her poems, translations, reviews and articles appear in numerous journals, including *The American Poetry Review*, *The Georgia Review*, *Poetry International*, *Pleiades*, *New Letters*, *Prairie Schooner*, *TriQuarterly*, *Arts & Letters* and *Mississippi Review*. She is the recipient of a 2011 Glenna Luschei Award from *Prairie Schooner* and a 2012 Individual Artist Award from the New Jersey State Council on the Arts. Moscaliuc was born and raised in Romania. She teaches at Monmouth University and in the M.F.A. Program in Poetry and Poetry in Translation at Drew University.

author photo: Mark Ludak

PORTRAIT

I thicken coffee with chocolate,
language with accented mistranslations,
love with foreign words
oblong and trammeled and plum-brandied.

I like the smell of yesterday's clothes.
It insists we resume where we left off.

BLOOD ORANGES FOR EASTER

Romania, 1980s

We secure our spot in line with three-hour shifts:
father plays chess, mother trades rumors,
grandma sees that no late arriver sneaks in.
When the truck doors snap open, we recognize
the crates. Each orange nests in crinkly tissue,
an extravagance so out of place we don't blink
when scales sink under heaps of cellophane.

But these oranges differ from the Christmas
imports: skins soused in blood,
as if birds have thrashed inside. We bag our fruit
in silence. The empty-handed do not protest.
At home, I dissect each sliver, stare at the meat
hewn with uneven patches of red, bite into the plump
striations, savor the pleasantly bitter juice.

Mother lets me take three segments to school,
but makes me promise to keep them out of sight.
We were lucky. You saw how few crates, so no teasing.
At lunch, my deskmate discovers the delicacy
balanced on my knees—"You can't eat that!
It's filled with blood!" he hisses, flapping bread-and-butter.
"That gypsy blood will kill you."

ODE TO FIRST LIES

Once you've tasted blood you can never stop,
Father says, as the dog goes down and I watch,
unsure of what comes next, how to bury
one killed with your own hands,
how to mourn, how to replace.

Only dogs, I repeat to myself, only dogs
can never stop.

LEILA TIME

We swim back at noon to rejoin from afar
the octopus who'd stunned us dumb.
Tentacles fraught with eerie grace
flutter and entangle, then halt, outstretched.
I can't read your eyes behind the fogged-up mask,
but decipher apprehension
in the way your fingers kiss my palm,
the way each stroke seismographs
the fierce intelligence that holds us still.

As you release my hand to capture
the creature through your fancy zoom,
its tentacles grow into Leila's fingers
curling with frightening precision,
straddling each other till the four tips almost touch—
but her thumb remains erect,
pointing outward to intercept some trill
or frequency beyond our hearing,
dowsing for direction, tentative yet unresigned.

Leila's hand seeks solitary passages
into consoling gardens of pure sound.
I press my thumb against her thumb,
almost at ease now with this nightly digression,
attuned to repeat this lullaby-like gesture
till Leila stops, signaling time's up.
Only this night her hand's artfully contorted butterfly
stays pressed against my thumb.
Leila's night, I think she means, as she lulls me
toward her bed, toward her time,
among exquisite, otherworldly butterflies.

THE REVENGE OF THE TONGUE

Found them waiting in clumps,
our winter's virginal knells.
Three milk-clotted lobes flared
to reveal the trim of petticoats.

Mouth full of woodsy snow,
I tongue-traced the hooded spathe,
three-celled ovaries, six-toothed anthers,
bit into the curving pedicel.

My tongue ached but I kept reaching back.

I did not hear your red boots
widen my footprints as they crossed the yard.
Galanthus Galatea, "*goddess of calm seas,*" "*milky white*"
—*one of the less common species*, you remarked,

and I'm still trying to forgive you.

LENA, THE HAIRY ORB, THE REBELS

Lena, unmarried neighbor, marches in armed
with blocks of wax and paint brushes, smacks
scarlet kisses on my cheeks, rolls thickly kohled eyes,
cursing the factory "rats" who stripped her
to check for stolen fabric. The first Saturday
of the month: my brother and father invent errands
for themselves, and soon more neighbors
arrive with gifts of razor, camphor, bruised apricots.
Sprawled naked on flowery pillows,
the women sip coffee and nibble rum rosettes,
praising each other's flesh—each gained gram
a measure of sly networking or culinary ingenuity.
They swap sugar, nail polish, condoms, smuggled spandex,
chuckle as they test the firmness of each other's breasts,
slather nipples and faces with raw honey and fruit purees.
Lena swears the best rejuvenator's semen and wants to start
a business. She half-jokes I'll marry "a Sagittarius with penis rising,
who knows, maybe even an American." Meanwhile, she says,
she'll sew me a "knock-out bikini" for I'm already "sprouting."
Fourteen, I can't bear to touch my body and loathe mirrors.
Mother hefts in the bubbling cauldron—ribbons of pale sap
raid the skin, uprooting resurgent colonizers: eyebrow stumps,
stiff blades, fine hairlings, "ewe down" of lush pubes.
I squeeze the bristly belts of wax into a globe and smooth continents
with sweaty fingers. When nobody watches, I smell
the future: frankincense, honeybees recaulking hives,
a hint of dizzying sweetness . . . but the camphor cork's off,
the 100W bulb's burning, and Lena's steaming
pot of chamomile hovers now under my blemished face.

SUICIDE IS FOR OPTIMISTS, CIORAN SAID

for Isabela V. (d. 1988)

1988. March. We do not leave the mortuary vault.
At night we huddle on spread blankets
As we did at the rock concert the summer before.
We drink from plastic bottles, cheap wine,
To celebrate the sexy quiver of your lip, the shifty curvature,
The ember ghost of each flaunted lisp.
Lascivious tongue: oyster slit *metaphoring what*, you had asked.
Ambrosian tongue: *changing despairs like workshirts*.
Viperine tongue: fangs loaded with subversive jokes.

When we blacklist the teachers who threaten
To fail us if we attend the funeral—
Suicide is the ultimate insult
to our harmonious communist life—
You wink in approval. We rise
On numb toes to kiss your eyelids.
We do not leave the mortuary vault
For three days. March. 1988.

I MET HER ONCE, WHEN I WAS EIGHT: IONUT SPEAKS

Halaucești orphanage, Romania

It was an ordinary morning: bread
with plum marmalade, nettle tea,
washroom smeared in citrine yellow,
toilet brush scrubbing our backs
purple. Ordered to the principal's office,
I take my time with the stairs, imagine

belt, rolling pin, willow stick ready
in his hand. *Your mother*, he says,
eyebrows arching to acknowledge the woman
sitting on a stool wedged behind the door, and I shake
my head. *Your mother*, he repeats, now parting
the curtain to catch a shout in the courtyard

and I shake my head. Wool headscarf
in scorching sun, doubled in front, mud-nosed
galoshes peeking under peasant skirt, and in her lap
a hen, a chick really, scrawny and dazed.
She lifts the bird toward me, without speaking—
her eyes, my own, follow me through the door,

down three flights. That night I roll the mouth
of a broken balloon up my left arm, and tightness
feels good, a warm compress, before the flesh
starts to swell and turn blue, then numb.
Can't say why, but I take hold of my limp wing
with the good one and lift it to my face, tenderly.

ALIEN RESIDENT

My mother rescues bitter cherries off Queens Boulevard.
She catches and hoists them in the net of her pleated skirt,
cradles them to her employer's kitchenette.
On a leather barstool that spins into night, she pits and pits,
keeps pace with the vermicular fanfare, bitter blood
under nails, petite castanets cackling in the dry mouth.
On the trenches of dawn, crushed flesh dissolves in the sugar bath
as she nods, on one elbow, to the squeals of bedroom doors.
She spoons coffee, keeping count aloud, and pours milk for kids' pancakes
as instructed, with a measuring cup. The perfect scale of her eyes
she wastes on homespun sanitizers—2/3vinegar 1/3 peroxide—
for sinks, counters, her Eager Beaver, his dumbbells.
She jogs through the day in bark slippers, mother dear, elm
embossed with perfectly knifed hearts.
What's she doing here, my mother, in a toddler cot, apron pockets
lined with shriveled fruit worms, jars of preserve
ticking under the mattress like hand grenades.

SELF-PORTRAIT WITH MONK

A bearded bride in black chiffon, lei of garlic dandling
his neck like the pearl ballroom choker of God,
he prances across the cobbled path, pushing a wheelbarrow
stacked with freshly scissored lovage and marigold.

I've been spying all morning from the terrace suspended
mid-wall and when, halfway across the courtyard, my monk lifts
his head, I abandon Eco's *In the Name of the Rose* and bend
over the wooden rail to flip a ladybug, sure he'll notice my silky mane.
He doesn't, so I trail through the oak door into the dining hall,
find him arranging frisky sunheads and mauve field tulips in clay pots.

I have already retraced the salty route of his fingers on the spines
of pickled grape leaves, in ground lamb hand-rolled in herbs sun-dried.
He cooks and feeds and scrubs but never eats, my monk,
spends lunch elbow-deep in suds or scratching the bellies of cats.

No wonder he's so famished by the time Cassiopeia arrives.
Then black chiffon and ivory flesh stream upwards,
shape-shifting in flight: raven, whiskered bat, *pricolici, vârcolac.*
At dawn, he lands between two rose bushes, soot in his mouth,
weeping who knows why, my celestial monk,
torn cassock glistening with spent saliva, rapture in upturned eyes.

IDRA NOVEY

Idra Novey is the author of *Exit, Civilian*, selected by Patricia Smith for the 2011 National Poetry Series and named a Best Book of 2012 by *Coldfront* and *The Volta*. Her first book, *The Next Country*, was a finalist for *Foreword*'s 2008 Book of the Year Award in poetry. In 2012, she received the Friends of Literature Award from the Poetry Foundation for poems which appear in *Clarice: The Visitor*, a chapbook of poems about houseguests, translation and syntactic breakdowns. Her work has been featured on NPR's *All Things Considered*, the *Leonard Lopate Show*, and in *Slate*, *The Paris Review*, *A Public Space* and *Poetry*. She teaches in the Creative Writing Program at Princeton University.

AUBADE FOR VIÑA DEL MAR

I follow a stray dog
so he'll stop following me
and a violin begins forming
in the pockets of my coat.

I have no ear for tuning
but it is six a.m.
and I will soon be the owner
of a complete instrument.

Now it's almost seven o'clock
and a torso of wood
is pressing into my side.
In the other pocket, the poke
of a bow.

EAST OF HERE

In the next country over, the lotus
is chocolate brown and grows tall

as maize. The sole religion seems
to be bread, any kind, including

one similar to rye, but made of lotus.
And if someone you've doted on

dies there defending
the nation, seven emissaries

for the president come by,
all wearing stethoscopes,

and listen to your heart. Afterward,
they offer artichoke sandwiches

in official blue Saran wrap and hand you
a list of either answers

or questions, but never both.
There's a road if you want to go.

DEFINITION OF STRANGER

Person not a member
of a group. A visitor,
guest, or the breast
that brushes your arm
on the subway. Person
with whom you've had
no acquaintance but who's taken
your rocking chair
from the curbside
and curls up in it
and closes her eyes.
Person in line
behind you now, waiting
for a glass of water,
of whiskey, or elixir.
Person logging on-line
at the same second
from the Home Depot in Lima
or in search of the Dalai Lama.
Person not privy or party
to a decision, edict, etcetera,
but who's eaten
from the same fork
at the pizzeria
and kissed your wilder sister
on New Year's. Person assigned
to feed the tiger at the zoo
where you slipped your hand
                                    once
into the palm
of somebody else's father.

A HISTORY IN SIX COUPLETS

Called a bird, the distant
dying city died as a bird does.

Dogs circled it, gray mud
caked on their haunches.

And all around,
a kind of tilting.

All around, chunks of concrete
like torn bread.

When asked about hunger,
the children replied with hunger.

When asked about birds,
they opened their mouths to the sky.

TIKAL

after Adam Zagajewski

I walked the forsaken city
in the rainy season

or the long light
of summer. I was obvious

or invisible, with no compass,
just this dogged pull—my kinship

with ruins. I could slip
on the wet stone steps

of Temple V
and disappear from here

as the Mayans did, or reach
the bottom again, go on to fall

from the flotsam
of some other empire.

It was dusk
or almost noon

and veins of black ants
pulsed on the fallen branches.

A MAÇA NO OSCURO

The story is like this: a man arrives
at the sorry farm of two sisters.

They hire him on the condition
that he sleep in the barn. A few chickens

bicker in the grass and before long
both women are in love. In my sleep,

I am the sister who slips
into that unsteady dark, finds her way

through the stink of animals,
past the bales of hay to the stranger.

Or it happens I am the one who stays
in bed, must listen to the other

crossing the yard. And I am left
with my swept room, my body

fixed in its place like a cabinet.
Either way, the intricacies of choice

are devouring. Either way, I wake
and do not recognize my life.

THE CANDIDATE

When falsely accused
of dishonesty, a woman
may slip into a hallway
and stroke the husk of curtain
over the closest window,
the sloping musty fringe of it.

If there's no curtain,
she may stroke the glass.

If it lacks a window,
she may lean into the wall
and imagine one, crawl out of it
onto a small boat
in a covert pond.

Rowing across,
she may rub at the reproach
like a stone in her palm,
consider tossing it waterward
or let it settle in her pocket.

She may grow dishonest,
become a rambler, pants sagging
with every manner of stone.

MEANWHILE THE WATERMELON SEED

On Tuesday, new prisoners arrive.

In late fall, when leaves clog the gutters and their last colors go out like stars, new prisoners arrive.

As another plane pitches upward and a red finch drops for landing.

As fleets of schoolchildren go forth in pursuit of green candy.

At three a.m., when dogs shift position on the bed and stir their owners who look out and find it's snowing.

In the hour when I call my sister and she empties the dishwasher, new prisoners arrive.

In the hour when drivers click on their headlights and flowers close and fireflies get trapped in jars.

On the evening when I see no one, read nothing, and somehow the hours are gone.

In the sweltering city, where a friend brings a watermelon and we spit its seeds onto the roof of the museum next door and the world seems repairable and temporarily right, new prisoners line up outside a pair of doors, enter one at a time.

RECENT FINDINGS

after the cells of Louise Bourgeois

I

Studies show the difference between legs and arms is in what tends to come after them: hands or feet. As the difference between teaching in a prison and the Ivy League is a question of attendance and if you can tell the weather from the wall.

II

This tiny spiral staircase in the corner appears to be moving. Some experts say it is not. They say getting a degree in prison is like this.

III

It's not uncommon, doctors concur, that gnawing on a stone while speaking of clauses to a mother and daughter incarcerated in the same prison may lead to gnawing that stone to stone.

IV

Recent polls note a breakdown in language when people say incarceration over generations, a hesitation and.

V

Too many enclosures make people cold, new data shows, and when it's cold it's going to be cold. As for the spider, she's feeling for an open seam between the walls.

CIVILIAN EXITING THE FACILITIES

Each week my body is fist-stamped and triple-scanned before it lands again
in the electoral world. My mind takes longer to leave, stays in the elevator
considering the kind of crime it might be capable of. Would I have to be
hungry. Could it happen over nothing. Could it happen nightly. In the shine of
a car outside the prison my reflection gets wider until it splits. In one likeness
the face I recognize. In the other my face.

RACHEL RICHARDSON

Rachel Richardson, whose first book is *Copper-head,* has received fellowships from the National Endowment for the Arts, Sewanee Writers' Conference, and Wallace Stegner Program at Stanford University. She currently teaches at University of North Carolina at Chapel Hill.

author photo: David Roderick

NOCTURNE: BENTON, LOUISIANA

There are places in this world telescopic and strange,
the dark like a power line—a thin grid sings its single note, falling
into my hair, across my back, netting me down
in some wide field. This would be mine: wet razor grass,
moonlight's new country, heat
nestled in leaves.

My father's voice, low, sacred, haunts me
the way wisteria curls into the burnt sharecroppers' cabins,
still here, and wraps the old headboards, floods
across cots. Each word humming, held—

NATCHEZ TRACE, SOUTHBOUND

On my windshield, the tiny backs
of insects break. The bleak
gravel heart of the crossroads
lifts its diamond sign, yellow,
its cross a split black eye.

Startled animals gleam
at roadside, each a study in vanishing.

When a squirrel darts
into my path, its eyes too low to warn,
I hear my breath more
than its crush. Barely a noise
to name me for certain.
But I am only passing;
the world keeps its silence.
No one blames me for a thing.

THE REFRAIN

I am learning, with the dark hand guiding mine,
    how to enter the small body of fig, how to scoop the flesh

in one motion, bring it to the bowl, cupped
    from its leather case—garnet, quivering.

I see the folded hand around mine, dry ridges,
    the heavy plain. I feel its press

and loosening, the way into skin, the excavation
    of fruit, egg-seeds and all. And it's this moment

when my grandmother enters—I never remember
    what was said, only the look of her in the doorway,

the eyes I thought for a moment were slit
    even when they were open. I won't recall gestures, or

the way Lola looked, hands in the air above her,
    pulled away from mine, mouth probably closed, no spot

on that white uniform. The figs like fish eyes
    upturned in the bowl. Their peeled skins collapsed and wet.

PORTRAIT OF BRITNEY SPEARS, KENTWOOD, 1996

From the first it was Let's pretend
                    and the game had a beat behind it,
          sinewy and breathing. She belted praises

in the Baptist choir. The Latin boys
                    at the Quick Stop watched her walk,
          and her math teacher leaned close

to her desk, examining her proof.
                    She smelled like watermelons, blushed
          when they voted her prettiest in school.

And Britney in the bathroom: oh the girls
                    crowded her even while she glossed
          her lips. The agent told her mother

she'd be a symbol of the New South,
                    and took her to a dogtrot house
          for the shoot. She'd brought her own

pink halter, whose ties she knew
                    brushed her bare skin when she moved.
          She understood his vision right away:

she should grasp the whitewashed
                    column like a pole,
          hold it like she'd never left

her home. He said Just pretend
                    you're a prisoner, or a slave, yes, yes,
          and keep your eyes right here.

CHILDREN BORN AFTER THE WAR

Somewhere on the road is everything you want:
cantaloupe, okra, roast peanuts overflowing
their bags. Muscadine jelly and moonshine
syrup, each in a heavy glass jar.
Everything rises: mayhaw choked by cane.

Thank your rubber tires and the smooth coins
in your palm. Thank your grandfather
and his battalions of boys. The road here
to Tulsa is lined with track. And each bright
fruit you tongue out of its shell
comes as if on air—no trace of origin, no thorn.

BLUES

Even the black is blue.
Even the cargo ship, a shrimp or lobster
boat or bigger, black-blue

against the fog and cerulean water.
And the boys and girls running in the water:
bruise-glowed, five-fingered outlines paused

like bent stars, kicking at the icy
froth of water, crouching for a blue-striped
beachball. It's that line in the back,

above the water and below the fog
that draws my eye—only because
the rest of the picture is so blue does this low air

appear white. A hollow-lostness white,
a pull to something distant, let's say.
Truly it is blue, as wet and deep-evening

as the ocean, the sand, the steamer, the beachball,
or the boys or the girls or the shine of the picture
glossing all their faces to blue.

Only my want for contrast invents it white—
as when given so much of one good thing
my eye searches for the lack.

AUDUBON AT OAKLEY PLANTATION

I need them true to life
and so I shoot them,
as many as fill the field at dawn,
and then fix wires
to prop them as if feeding their young
or bending to the river.

Why make a little book
when they exist life-sized,
can be etched to stand high as my hip?
Often have I wished
I had eight pairs of hands to hold them,
and another body for the gun.

NAVIGATOR

       Imagine having no destination—not the Friendly
Center or aquarium—but journeying only
to find a *usable route*, like Captain Cook:
adrift until currents pushed you
into a certain lane, certain highway with its humpbacked
traffic bobbing along—
       your young not strapped in the back flinging
Cheerios into the crevices like a game of skeet
but moored in the house with mother
so you could seek your destiny here—

       Imagine stewing the bones a fourth time
to leach any last juice into your meager
broth—not the pirate birthday cake
with seafoam-colored frosting, nor the drive-thru;
not the Frosty, not the McRib—
       placenames still to be scrawled,
held in your mouth new-minted
to mark this passage, its weather and bits of luck.

       The usable route: a velvet highway you trace
onto parchment, not the GPS lady recalculating—
       a way to inscribe *we are not lost* in a vast expanse
of lostness, not the road signs and,
sold everywhere, the smartphones gleaming.

PLATH'S CAKES

A dough spirals,
                    making itself
from the assembled
ingredients, which

          once together
cannot be separated.
Work done right in the rising
and browning—
                         but
the multiplication of them
taunts her,
the countertop counting.

Heat: a chamber
to bind them.

          It could be said
there were signs. The sea
howled its hollow song.

And it could be said the hawk
with the mouse
          not in its talons
but held in its mouth, alive,
was the inevitable grasp—

(and pens
on the desk, muddy shoes
by the door)

          the hook and glove
together, the bedposts rooted
in the upstairs room.

WHALE-STUDY

When they go down, they are
unreachable. The distance beyond light
only tells their route by the scars
they bear back to the surface.
In such depths night opens,
breathes, unsplit by rays
of sun. A quiet snow falls;
hatchetfish lower their jaws.
So many nights I have wept
for the city of my childhood,
imagining it sunk—but for them
there is no floor,
here past the shore-hugging tides,
wrecks glittering with rust
still oozing rainbows upward—

they go down hunters, blind.
Memory is a map. Midnight
presses deep in their mammalian hide.

ANNE MARIE ROONEY

Anne Marie Rooney is the author of *Spitshine*,
as well as the chapbooks *The Buff* and *Shell of
an egg in an effort*. Her work has been featured
in the *Best New Poets* and *Best American Poetry*
anthologies, and received the *Gulf Coast* Prize
in Poetry, *The Iowa Review* Award, a Barbara
Deming Grant and others. A founding member
of Line Assembly, she currently lives in New
Orleans, where she works as a teaching artist.

author photo: Lillian-Yvonne Bertram

WHAT MY HEART IS TURNING

My heart. My heart a black flower. Not that. And is my heart an arrow
when in the morning it is crowing. My heart, my heart's crowing,
in the morning there is a blackness to the crowing of my heart. If in the morning
it wakes you. If the sky is black and then it is not black, if the sky travels up
from black and then if my heart is too loud. My heart is awake. If my heart is awake
then my heart is too loud. If in the morning my heart is too loud and it wakes you
and your muffled eyes open and there, there is my heart in the middle of the room.
Or my heart is at the window, crowing and crowing. Then do not touch it
but watch it. So when the sky has traveled its distance
from black and then dark and then not dark and then pink, then,
when my heart has spent its restless quiver. Touch it. Touch my heart so
it burns. Turn and lean forward out of the bed, enter the room and touch my heart
like fire (this black flower, this fever, this pitch, this scrubbed clean, this arch
of morning, this riding night, this black pitch, this fever, this book
in the mouth, this bird in the city, this siphon, this is prisoning, this fever, this pitch,
this mouth on the shelf, this bed on the back, this black city, this arch of bird,
this morning in the mouth, this woman riding night, this pitch
of fire, this bird from the prison, this shelf of fever, this back is not clean,
this arch in the chapter, this book in the morning, this pitch, this fever, this city's
on fire), be fearless, touch me and that turning sun

DOMESTIC

In the time it takes to set the line, each keyplace
has become vague. In the first, every stone stops
a look. Further christened, the damn door gap holds
a curvature but even we now-met won't revisit that low
clef corner. There there is a horrible face only ended
on the curb. Like paper we cut our gait
from impossible tetrises. Become creatures
that barb the night. Creatures who.

FLOWER SONNET

The way bravery tails out sharply like
the staunch come-on, creature of more wanting
even than me. When we met, my wanting
him was tangential to the pinch. It's like
my mother said before she slumped in: like
it or like its petals. Even wanting
turns over. The way I opened, wanting
more even than him. And so I was like
the stinger already having scooped whole
pits. How does need, and can it really be
crossed under? This well from which oh my whole
me-ness shakes down. If hot is what he'll be
I'll spread a honey too. Two can play bee
to that pluck. Even smarting is a hole.

ELEGY IN WHICH I SLEEP RESTFULLY

This is the story that keeps giving: In
      the middle of the winter I become
            unknown to myself. Yes, there's still the hum
of cup after cup: the water boils, gin is poured,
            drunk. I pickle sweetly. My tin heart opens its bag
      of hope, asks for company, beats like a hurricane
of subways. In this city of hard winds, I undress slowly
            before the window, see the shadow
            of smoke from my hot room opening
      against the next building and do not think
anything, go out walking and do not speak to anyone
            about it. The room of this feeling grows
      larger, swells until it can be taken in
            without teeth, like vegetables water-
            warped for hours. I unbolt myself, feed the cat.
      When my lover comes to me I have made myself
            a minor thing. In the evening, I take his lips
      in mine, use that word, *hell*, tell him I will not
            keep. Outside this moment, another room calls
                  me, calls for the wall of my chest to fill
            again with air. Elegy in which a slow heart.
                  Elegy in which poached song. From the scar
                  of this feeling I take another swill.

ELEGY IN WHICH THE FILM DEGRADES

1

She has seen the angle a man shudders into.
The slab of haunch a promise. This woman
whose face opens like a butcher's knot.
"Both my daughters know how to grieve,"
she says, but something beats against
this. Past the window, a blind of rain and dirtier.
If tonight I flatten to a list. "Shabby and hot"
is what she called me, and then I showed her real fire.

2

So this arrow opens its fever: Where there is one
cut there are five. To say nothing of the light
is to say nothing of how a dead room can warp
cankers into lovers. The thickness of sickness
swelters and under its skin. Still the beauty
of the body's swollen crown. All its gilded
mars.   Peel back the spears, the bitter thistle.
        Eat the oily heart.

3

The slab of haunch a promise: a slow answer
takes hold. By hour's end, what is left of her story
will turn clean. What is left
will turn the water at the bed
of the one who breaks into wave.
Tell it like this:
The yarn of the body unravels. Then the body
unravels.

2.
I look out from my spire of fuss and buzzkill. A carriage is awaking on the hill.
The sun shifts and maybe it is you come for the annual tap. Last year you rode
right up and with your spurs aglitter clicked your tongue. Did you think I was a
home? I would buckle under you? I look again and the angle of everything has
changed. There is no sun here and I am the sun, that starched, appalled. The
something I have become
is truly unbecoming.

5.
Your wink sugars down my spine. I think: I want to take a bath. I think: Am I a
red bulb or am I something lower. For hours I do nothing
but talk to the squall. The many whistles of bird through water become one
dull hum, which I stop hearing two cloudbreaks in. Though
the room is dark I shutter it, sit in the dark, am dark with a dark
hole. I should never call myself
a hole.

3.
On the third day I feel a start in my middle scar—there is no word but the word
for anger, the revolting dog lapping rough and everywhere. If I am this sharp
I would rather not be. I preen the feathers of your tribute, and they sag
forward. Dulled luster, I would rather be prone than hard-won.

4.
All I got's this window, this turning red. Through the night, it holds itself
between me and blacker. It saves my hide. It keeps me hidden. In this it is like
a skin, but it is not your skin, your sweet and cold and blue. The things I
would do if I had you for a shoe.

1.
The hero thought me wicked
His mother made me moan
I shot shotguns
I rode shotgun
I never went home

INSTRUCTIONS FOR WOOING ME
(MONSTER THAT I AM)

First generate a charge. Rub hard if you have to. Crash a little against
my fleeciest spots. When I begin to stain with electricity, turn your faucets
off. I am a pornography of small promises. I tell you this softly because really
I am a soft thing. I open my modesty umbrella. This is how you know to get out
your cutting board. If I balk pull a tooth or two. I want you to do this to me
because I want you to do this. I am the chugging gin of the universe. I balm
and bomb. In your mind I burn like thirty watts of unstrained honey.
I am not very bright with my antennae on. With diamonds
and things that are less than diamonds on. Like a lone languid
heat storm, you say. I say The ribcage is not a sensible machinery.
But I am dimmer even than the face of a leap year. Stop me if I start
to speak of terror. It is a habit unbecoming of being here. It is not good
for your sauna perspective. Is my surge protector paling? I pale
to speak of it. In the jar rimmed with pollen is a knife with your name on it.
Have I told you about the big development? You are dreaming
of me now. If I am glowing like a firefly know that I am not
a firefly. This time of night every bee dusts with a little sparkling blow. Blow me
back to the square I came from. It's your move, I say. You move an inch
away. Step seven: I turn red as a city. Step eight: I become a little less
uniform. I sprout seven more whiskers. I hiss like a fire house
expelling its heroes. You know what to do. I can tell by your glasses.
If map then midriff. If shot glass then novocaine. That will be all
my surnames on the floor. I'm fair game, Joe. It's always open season
on princesses.

WHAT THE HEART RECOVERS

Swallow of the filter. Which falls upon you like
A burning rafter. This happened. Seminary books
Destroyed. No one thanked you
For your sweet mystery. Which swelled within them
As pollen within a pipe: soon all the taps
Sung golden with that flower. It's not that
Romantic: swallow it
Before more doves can drown in your line, or the stolen
Silk shed onto the wood in slow puddles.
At night naked the only water isn't wet, not
Really. Press that blowy photograph against your heart
Neck chest. It can light a drying fire, too, the burnish
In the less, then lost, then one last lens dressed gamely
In a red to stitch a nun to sleep. There is no picture for this:
Call the stoic what he is, expanding starch
Souring its own gluey waters. You were that water once, that yes
Steeping downwards into blue. He drew a little
Sherpa on your back. All signs pointed to the slack
Finger with which he traced your true. Black figure
Opening: this was you.

BUT ANIMALS EMBODY GENDER
EVEN AS THEY ARE BEYOND IT

Sliding down of towers, moon in tree. Men
surround me
in the early skin of my backache.
Moon in the water and landed grass
beholding. Down-sliding me
through each evening. Our boxes and down-sliding
towers, tree slickening
to cold. Oh moon, who cares
for your slick-sly down. The sky
when you slide drops down. Evening
skeins off in down-meaning
ropes. Body
with its mark. And stable,
surrounding. Grass upon which
a moon can cast light.
Circle of hold-me-down
light. Men
surround me
in the slide-downing sparrow. Little blow-bird with light
on its circle. A grass grows
the water darker. In flood the red knot
slips down. Silt on the moon making blood
and down-sliding towers, the men that
surround me. Arrow of men and bird never
reaching. Down the grass which
slickens the even-so. Evening, that stiff
skin, slacks off its crust.
Heart's open bag, slag on the water.
Men
surround me,
swell of water going
green. Down-sliding
to grass and landed
towers blue. Men
surrounded me next year,
too.

ELEANOR STANFORD

Eleanor Stanford is the author of two books of poetry, *The Book of Sleep* and *Bartram's Garden*, and the memoir *História, História: Two Years in the Cape Verde Islands*. Her poems and essays have appeared in *Poetry*, *Ploughshares*, the *Harvard Review*, *The Iowa Review* and others. She lives in the Philadelphia area.

PISGAH

We woke in the field
and found the fence down, nothing between us
and the cows. They were thinking deeply
about the grass. Their stomachs
four-chambered, like hearts.

Driving west into Tennessee, the fog
glittered like mica. The wedding glasses,
packed in paper, rattled in the trunk.
The words were all so inexact.

But years later, you said, remember the fog,
how it was like pressing the palm of your hand
to your closed eyelids until stars appeared,

and I said yes, I remembered it.

IDEOGRAM

Above the forked branch, sound
flutters like a swallow. We live
in the moment's wicker cage, its hanging
house open to the wind. Snow slants
against the pane, the blank grid recalling
rice fields in Hokkaido. You trace
the curve of my cheek—first brushstroke
of a difficult character. In Japan,
where scholars spend a lifetime
learning how to write, it is the simplest words
that are the test of mastery: the bent twig
of a man, the four uneven beats of the heart.

EZRA AT SIX WEEKS

Sleep, porous as cheesecloth,
lets light in. His cry a thin rope
that drags me up again and again.
Sun filters through the limbs
of the bur oak. Across the street
the Sudanese children wait
for the bus, poke the ground
with sticks, look injured.
What did they expect?
Not this. Certainly
not this.

MÁLAGA

The water flickers below the window.
Vines loose their fuchsia blossoms in my sleep,
and fog blooms across the pane.

All I remember is the words, how they moved like snakes,

shed their skin and glistened in the sun. The bay ripples,
spinning, an age-warped record.

A woman leans over the balcony, singing a bolero,
bright ribbons of sorrow trailing from her silk shawl.

The tide will swallow you until you learn
to let your body go, to swim back out on a pulse of blood.

THE BOOK OF SLEEP (XVIII)

You drove all night through thunderstorms, the PA turnpike
slick and narrow in the passes. The tractor trailers roaring,
and sleep
whistling past your ears. . . .

My heart was where a hundred roads
converged & then moved on

At one point you drove under a mountain.
Later the sun unfolded over the hills,
and you realized the rain had stopped.

You found me on the shore of Lake Erie.
At my feet a million prehistoric animals offered up
their calcified bodies.

Presque Isle, it was called.

We held hands in the dark theater. A woman read a book
in a sparsely furnished bedroom. Ants crawled across
an open palm.

Then you left, and again the dull sun, the clock
parceling out the hours. Again the nuns tending the gardens
in their sad habits.

THE BOOK OF SLEEP (XV)

All night I waited at the edge of the gallery-forest.
I dreamed the lion with your bloody cloak in his mouth.
I dreamed the river swallowed you, your body
a small bulge in its throat.

This place where I live now, it is a country
whose name has changed many times.
A country whose present status
is not clear.

By the sleek surface of the lake,
the cattle flick their tails,
bend their large heads to drink.

On the road I saw a beautiful girl,
carrying a clay urn on her head.
She balanced it so casually,
I knew it was full, and knew
that whatever it contained
was all she had.

LETTER IN JULY

We spent the afternoon sitting on a blanket on the floor,
fitting plastic cups inside each other, building a tower,
knocking it down. I heard Berryman's mother admonishing,
"To confess you're bored means you have no Inner Resources."
And my own mother, when I was bored:
"Go bang your head against the wall."

Summer is another thing. Humid and dumbstruck, we return
to childhood. We walk the dog. We feed the chickens. In the
                                                    evening,
a thunderstorm beats the zucchini in the garden to the ground.
I am afraid of the suburbs, of their unearthly quiet,
rain-drenched hydrangeas blushing in the yard,
rusty nails buried at their roots.

In a Palestinian poem, I find the line, *Farewell,*
small island of ours.

Today I fed the baby his first taste
of solid food. I mixed rice cereal with breast milk
and lifted it on my finger to his mouth. The flakes a lunar confetti
scattered in the bowl. He made a face and swallowed:
half celebration, half a spoonful of regret.
Farewell, small island of ours.

When Berryman jumped from a bridge in Minnesota,
his name billowed out behind him like a cape. But did not stop
his fall. If he did not think of his mother in Oklahoma,
I think of her now, rolling out biscuit dough, stamping it
into circles with a glass, confessing nothing.

POLITICAL POEM

While the President is speaking about security,
I am straining peas through the food mill, splattering
the kitchen counter with green specks. The radio is on
at a low volume, so I will be less tempted
to throw things at it, but instead I just grind harder,
until my fingers are pressed against
the metal holes, threatening to grate the skin
from my knuckles. If this were another country, somewhere
in Latin America, say, or Eastern Europe, I could write lines like,
My country, take care of your light!, as Neruda did,
I could write, *I am begging you the way a child*
begs its mother, as he did, staring out his window
at the ocean tiresomely reiterating on the black rocks.
Oh, to live among those writers
who make unabashed use of vodka
and exclamation marks! Except in such a place
I would probably be the one lost in the steam
of a pot of boiling cabbage, I would be the one
with a baby tied to her back and her hands
busy on the tortilla board, flattening anger
into perfect floured circles. As here in my kitchen full
of modern appliances, I push my anger through
the metal strainer, and prepare to feed it by small spoonfuls,
mixed with rice cereal and breast milk, to the baby.

CHILDREN

They hollow you out. Their colored plastic shovels
working, scraping the bottom
of the sandbox.

Still, you can't say it.

What are you doing? I ask my two-year-old.
My back turned, stirring something.
Playing with knives, he says. His enunciation
newly honed, proud blade.

Look out the window. The suburbs' orderly
paved quiet. The streets named for tribes
long since extinct.

Last week, when I left
a bone-handled knife on the stove,
and the flame caught, I stood there, mouthing
Fire. Fire. As though saying it
I'd set the house ablaze.

TWO COMMON DAFFODILS (*NARCISSUS PSEUDONARCISSUS*)

> *Oh hours of childhood, when behind each shape more*
> *than the past appeared, / and what streamed out before us*
> *was not the future.*
> —Rilke, "Fourth Elegy"

I ride backwards on the train, facing where I'm coming from, gritty town
of numbered streets, March with its muddy footprints, saying,
not so fast. The book on my lap illuminated in the window. Rilke
spread ghostly over the chemical plants of North Jersey, over the smoke
cocooning in the sky and disappearing. Rilke
and his adolescent longing no one leaves behind, except
in longing more.

We fought before I left. Now, the boys in bed,
you pour cachaça in a glass. Crush the ice
and lime, stir in the sugar with a knife.

Each intensifies the other—lime's bruised peel,
sugar echoing the ice's hard clarity.

The pleasure's in not yielding.

The light is slipping from the loading docks and storage lockers,
behind the pawnshops and the strip clubs. You enter our sons' room
to watch them sleeping. Mouths agape, limbs entwined.
On the dresser, in a tin can's makeshift vase, the flowers
I picked earlier, their bells drooping.

In the living room, you slip your parents' old record
from its sleeve. Stan Getz in his yellow starched lapels,
the saxophone's brass slouch. Even though it's dark,
I know these last few miles: marsh grass and mud,
and the long tunnel. You lower the needle. What streams out
is gently tongued regret, so many variations on a single note.